Vermeer *illuminated*

A report on the restoration of the *View of Delft* and

The Girl with a Pearl Earring by Johannes Vermeer

By Jørgen Wadum,

with contributions by René Hoppenbrouwers and

Luuk Struick van der Loeff

CONSERVATION,

RESTORATION AND

RESEARCH

V+K Publishing / Inmerc

Mauritshuis, The Hague

[1995]

Contents

Preface

1. Johannes Vermeer 1632-1675

2. Vermeer's painting technique

3. Conservation, restoration and research

      3.1 The Girl with a Pearl Earring

      3.2 View of Delft

4. Afterword

Notes

Bibliography

Further reading

In recent years visitors to the Mauritshuis and other museums in the Netherlands have shown a growing interest in conservation and restoration. This interest led to the development of the Delta Plan for the Preservation of the Netherlands' Cultural Heritage which in turn, generated further interest in conservation and restoration. Under the Delta Plan, developed by Hedy d'Ancona, the former Minister of Welfare, Health and Cultural Affairs, tens of millions of guilders have been made available in recent years for long overdue conservation work in museums in the Netherlands.

When such major activities are undertaken in the area of conservation, museum visitors are, naturally, entitled to more information. The *Vermeer Illuminated* restoration project carried out in the summer of 1994 and this publication aim to provide that information. The Rabobank provided financial support for the restoration work.

The main part of the *Vermeer Illuminated* project was the conservation and restoration of two paintings by Vermeer in the collection of the Mauritshuis. The *View of Delft* and *The Girl with a Pearl Earring* are among the best of Dutch art from the Golden Age. The paintings had been in need of treatment for some time, for aesthetic as well as conservation reasons. During the restoration, the clouded and discoloured varnish as well as discoloured retouches and overpaintings were removed from the two Vermeers. This restoration work has now revealed the brilliant colours and subtle nuances of these two masterpieces.

These restorations also provided an opportunity to study the techniques used in the paintings. The information gleaned from such technical studies is now increasingly valued. As a result of greater interdisciplinary cooperation between art historians, conservators and scientists, technical information about painting methods is now more widely included in catalogues and monographs about artists. During the restoration of these works, all aspects of Vermeer's technique were studied and will be presented at the Vermeer exhibition to be held at the Mauritshuis in the spring of 1996.

Since the Mauritshuis did not want to take the Vermeers from view for a prolonged period, it was decided to undertake the restoration work in full view of the public. Hence, the museum set up a temporary restoration studio. This also provided an opportunity to give the public a chance to become more familiar with the

1

conservation and restoration of our cultural heritage, one of the most important aspects of contemporary museum management. Particularly as restorations are generally carried out behind closed doors.

The restorations were undertaken in consultation with an international support committee. The need for restoration, research, conservation and the restoration work itself, were all discussed in detail. The members of the committee were the restorers David Bomford (National Gallery, London), Viola Pemberton-Pigott (The Royal Collection, London) and Dr Hubert von Sonnenburg (The Metropolitan Museum of Art, New York) and the art historians Professor Egbert Haverkamp Begemann (New York University), Dr Arthur K Wheelock (National Gallery of Art, Washington) and Professor Ernst van de Wetering (Amsterdam University).

The restoration of the *View of Delft* was carried out by Luuk Struick van der Loeff. *The Girl with a Pearl Earring* was cleaned by Jørgen Wadum and retouched by Nicola Costaras. The background research on Delft painting techniques in the period of Vermeer was undertaken by Koos Levy-van Halm. We would like to express our thanks to Karin Groen, Stichting Restauratie-Atelier Limburg in Maastricht, the Central Research Laboratory for Objects of Art and Science in Amsterdam, DSM Research in Geleen and the FOM Institute of Atomic and Molecular Physics in Amsterdam for the analyses of the samples. Han Geene and Ed Brandon provided the photographic documents. The X-ray photographs of the *View of Delft* were done by the Röntgen Technische Dienst in Rotterdam. The temporary restoration studio was designed by Archipel architects and C. Marreloo of the Government Buildings Agency. We would also like to thank all the staff of the Mauritshuis, particularly the internal services department, who supported the conservators throughout the project.

F.J. Duparc

1 Forecourt of the Mauritshuis during the restoration open to the public.

2 The public restoration studio.

2

5

3

1. JOHANNES VERMEER 1632-1675

Vermeer was born in Delft in 1632. His grandparents were refugees from Antwerp. His father was an innkeeper who also traded paintings from his inn, the 'Mechelen'. After his training, in 1653 Johannes Vermeer became a member of the painters' guild of St Luke in Delft at the age of twenty-one. It is not known who his teacher was, but Leonard Bramer has been suggested as he was a friend of Vermeer's parents and was a witness at Vermeer's wedding. It is likely that Vermeer was also influenced by Carel Fabritius because in 1667 Vermeer was compared in a poem with this talented painter also working in Delft. From 1662 to 1670 Vermeer was headman of the Guild of St Luke which suggests that he was already recognised during his lifetime. However, he did not set out to establish himself as a painter. He took over the inn from his father and sold and valued paintings. This is how he provided for his family which, by this time, included eleven children.

Only some thirty paintings can be attributed to Vermeer with any certainty. It is unlikely that he had any apprentices as painting was not his main profession.[1]

Johannes Vermeer was buried in the Oude Kerk in Delft on 15 December 1675. He left his widow and eight children destitute.

The *View of Delft* (96.5 x 115.7 cm) was probably painted around 1660, a few years after *The Little Street*, now at the Rijksmuseum in Amsterdam.[2] This is Vermeer's only other known exterior painting. Vermeer painted Delft seen from the other side of the Schie river. The view includes the medieval ramparts demolished in the 19th century, the Schiedam Gate in the centre and the Rotterdam Gate on the right. Ships are moored at the quayside. The clock on the Schiedam Gate indicates a time between seven and half past seven.[3] In the distance the tower of the Nieuwe Kerk can be seen above the rooftops.

6

4

3 *The Little Street* (54.3 x 44), Rijksmuseum, Amsterdam.
4 *View of Delft* (96.5 x 115.7), Mauritshuis, after the 1994 restoration.

In 1921 Proust wrote, 'After seeing a view of Delft in a museum in The Hague, I realised I had seen the most beautiful painting in the world'.[4] This further increased the reputation of this already well-known painting. The powerful, in some respects almost impressionistic, style of painting and the extraordinary representation of the light in the *View of Delft* are very rare in 17th century painting. Maxime du Camp, who saw the painting in 1859, wrote 'Van der Meer is an impressive painter who uses even colours over large, thick areas'.[5]

5

Although Vermeer is best known for his interiors his most valued painting is probably *The Girl with a Pearl Earring* (44.5 x 39 cm). This canvas was probably painted in 1665. A few years later he painted the *Portrait of a Young Woman*, now in New York.[6] These two paintings have many similarities. Both girls are looking at the viewer over their left shoulder. Both wear a yellow turban or headscarf which hangs down to the shoulder. *The Girl with a Pearl Earring*, now in The Hague, is a *tronie*, i.e. Vermeer did not paint a specific person but an idealized face. The headgear, which is not Dutch, confirms that the figure is fictional. Depicting men and women in exotic costumes was a popular painting genre in the 17th century. The inventory of Vermeer's estate specifically refers to '...a small *tronij* painting'.[7]

6

7

5 *The Girl with a Pearl Earring* (44.5 x 39),
Mauritshuis, after the 1994 restoration.
6 *Portrait of a Young Woman* (44.5 x 40),
Metropolitan Museum of Art, New York.

7 Structure of a painting on canvas.

7 varnish

6 glaze

5 paint layer

4 dead colour / underpainting

3 underdrawing

2 ground

1 size

0 canvas

8 *The Painter's Studio*, David Ryckaert III, Musée des Beaux-Arts, Dijon.

Introduction

Clearly, it would be impossible to give a complete overview of Vermeer's painting technique purely on the basis of the two paintings discussed here. Extensive investigations of all his works were needed to discover the methods he used in his studio. Questionnaires were sent to all the collections and museums housing paintings by Vermeer. This provided a great deal of information about Vermeer's technique in a relatively short time. This technical information was also used in the interpretation and restoration of the paintings at the Mauritshuis. All the information was studied in detail and recorded, and will be included in the exhibition catalogue to be published at a later date. However, this publication includes a foretaste of some of that information.

A study of Vermeer's oeuvre shows that his early works, in particular, were painted with fluid strokes using large brushes. His technique became more refined in later years. His paintings were also generally small. The two exceptions to this rule are the famous *Allegory of Painting*, in Vienna, and the *Allegory of the Faith*, in New York.[8]

The structure of the two paintings by Vermeer

17th century paintings are made up of a wide range of materials and several stages can be identified in the creation of these paintings. For example, painters had a choice of supports such as canvas, wood panels and copper. The support was prepared with size and several layers of ground. The painter would generally transfer his design to the support as an underdrawing. Once this was completed painting could start. The underpainting of the various areas would be undertaken carefully, after which they were completed with paint layers of various densities and degrees of transparency. Vermeer used oil paint. Painters used to make this paint by grinding linseed oil, the binding medium, with pigments, the particles which lend colour to the paint.

This painting depicts a 17th century painter's studio. To the right of the painter a man is grinding paint on a large slab. The background includes a canvas on a strainer similar to the original strainer of the *View of Delft*.[ill.8]

9

Support

The Girl with a Pearl Earring and the *View of Delft* are both painted on canvas. Vermeer generally preferred canvas. He only did two small paintings on panels, both in the National Gallery of Art in Washington. One of these cannot be attributed to Vermeer with absolute certainty.[9] However, the inventory of his estate shows that he did more paintings on wooden supports. The inventory refers to ten canvas paintings and six panels in the front room of his house.[10]

> In the 17th century painters' canvasses, usually made of linen, were secured with string to a strainer slightly larger than the piece of canvas. The canvas was then grounded.
> Tight stretching of the canvas would cause cusping because the canvas was less taut between the points where it was secured. This would lead to undulations parallel to the planks of the strainer. Cusping often extends 15 to 20 cm into the painting. [ill.8,9,10]

10

All the tacking edges and tacking holes of the *View of Delft* are still preserved. The canvas also has a selvage on two sides.
This shows that the width of the canvas is the same as the roll of linen used by Vermeer. The width of this roll was about 118 cm/4 Brabant feet, i.e. about 2 Brabant ell. The height of the canvas chosen by Vermeer is about 99 cm, or about 3.5 feet. The height to width ratio of this painting is 1:1.20.[11]
The width to height ratio of *The Girl with a Pearl Earring* is 1:1.14, a ratio similar to that of many other Vermeers. The size of the canvas, 44.5 x 39 cm, 1.5 x 1.3 feet, is the same as several other paintings by Vermeer from different periods. This cannot be due to chance. Rather, it suggests that Vermeer used standard sizes.

9

9 *Painter's Studio* (detail), Gonzales Coques, Staatliches Museum, Schwerin.
10 *Girl with a Pearl Earring* (X-ray detail): cusping.
11 *View of Delft* (detail): left selvage with cusping at the front. The dark brown lining adhesive is visible on the left of the canvas.
12 *View of Delft* (detail): right edge with brown ground beyond the painted area.

11

12

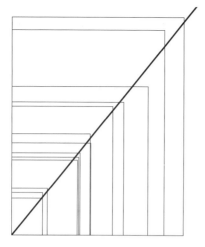

13

In Flanders standard canvas sizes were commonly used from the end of the 16th century. Standard sizes are known to have been used in the Northern Netherlands from the early 17th century.[12] The standard size used generally depended on the genre of the painting. For example, sea paintings were generally painted on narrow canvasses with a height to width ratio of about 1:1.60. However, landscapes often had a ratio of 1:1.40 and portraits a width to height ratio of 1:1.20.[13] This last ratio and the ratio of 1:1.14 often used by Vermeer suggest that he used almost exclusively portrait-size canvasses for most of his paintings. [ill.13]

Sizing and grounding

The stretched canvas was first coated with animal glue. The primary purpose of this was to protect the linen against penetration by the binding medium in the ground which followed. The ground generally comprised a mixture of chalk, glue and linseed oil. Pigments were often added. The ground of Vermeer's *The Girl with a Pearl Earring* was shown to contain lead white, black and a small quantity of red and brown ochre. The ground of the *View of Delft* not only contains chalk, lead white, black and red and brown ochre but also brown umber.[14]

17th century painters were aware of the effects of a coloured ground on the overall tone of paintings. The hue of the ground, warm or cold, is important particularly if it is overpainted with thin, transparent layers of paint.

For the *View of Delft* Vermeer used a warm, brown-grey colour. For *The Girl with a Pearl Earring* he used a cool grey ground.

To take an X-ray photograph, the painting is exposed to X-rays and the transmitted radiation which is not absorbed is then recorded on film. The image on the film is lighter in areas where the radiation is absorbed by the painting. The absorbtion depends on the nature and thickness of the materials. The X-ray photograph of The Girl with a Pearl Earring shows that the ground must have been applied with a knife, possibly one similar to the grounding knife illustrated in De Mayerne's treatise on painting from 1620.[15] The grounding paste was spread over the canvas in large arcs. The knife was dragged from right to left, along the top and then down along the left edge. A later movement from the bottom left upward is also visible. These movements can be deduced from the thicker areas of ground (these show up lighter on the X-ray photograph) which are always to the left of the stretching points where the knife was dragged across the canvas with less pressure than just before these points. [ill.14]

14

10

13 The ratios of Vermeer's paintings. The corners of paintings with the same length / width ratios lie along the diagonal.

14 *The Girl with a Pearl Earring:* X-ray and processed image. For grounding the canvas was stretched onto a larger strainer with string. The grounding knife was dragged along the top edge of the canvas.

15 *Allegory of Painting* (detail), Kunsthistorisches Museum, Vienna.
16 *View of Delft* (X-ray). The dead colour, which contains lead white, absorbs most of the X-rays. The view of the town, partly reserved in the dead colour shows up dark on the X-ray.

After grounding, a canvas was often transferred to a different strainer before painting. Originally these were fixed frames. From about 1750 stretchers become popular. These frames could be expanded with the wedges in their corners. This was used not only when stretching the canvas on the frame for the first time, but also later when the painting had lost its tension.

The underdrawing

No underdrawing could be identified with any certainty in either of these Vermeer paintings. The infrared imaging systems used for this purpose can only show underdrawings made in black. However, under a stereomicroscope some paint strokes in a light ochre colour could be detected on *The Girl with a Pearl Earring*, on the ground at the edge of the face. This may be a sketched underdrawing in paint. From the second quarter of the 17th century it was not unusual to sketch the composition in light ochre. For example, on Vermeer's *The Allegory of Painting* we can see how the painter made the underdrawing on the support in a light colour with a brush.[16]

It is likely that Vermeer did not develop the composition as an underdrawing but rather through underpainting. This could also explain why there are no known drawings or sketched designs by Vermeer.

Underpainting

In the method used by Vermeer the first stage in painting was to apply the dead colour (monochrome underpainting). In the 17th century this term referred to local development of the composition to indicate the light and dark areas. Certain areas – the underpainting – were then painted as the first layer on the dead colour.
Vermeer used the dead colour and underpainting very effectively and subtly. The colours of these layers, together with the ground and the final paint layers, determine the required tone. In the *View of Delft* he underpainted the sky with a simple layer of lead white on the brown ground. This provided the required cool tone of the blue sky. After this he could simply complete parts of the sky in blue and the clouds with yellows and greys. The light parts of the water and foreground also began with the dead colour using paint with lead white as well as grey, blue and yellow hues.
By contrast, the buildings were partly left open (reserved) and partly started in black dead colour. It could be that Vermeer used underpainting in colour for some of these areas.

15

16

11

17

17   *View of Delft:* By painting the cloud transparently over the gap in the blue, Vermeer used the white dead colour to keep the area in the centre of the cloud light.

18   *The Girl with a Pearl Earring:* blue turban after cleaning.

19   *The Girl with a Pearl Earring:* the girl's nose after cleaning.

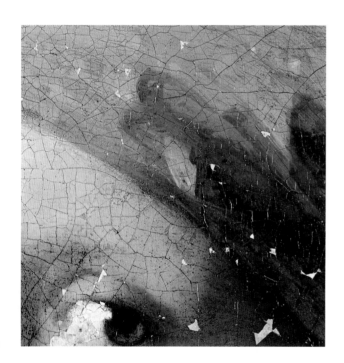

18

19

12

20

The dead colour has a decisive influence on the tone of *The Girl with a Pearl Earring* because Vermeer built up the various areas with thin layers of paint at a later stage.

> The shadows in the blue of the turban and on the jacket have black underpainting. The shadows on the face contain reds and browns. For example, the underpainting on the left of the nose contains red ochre, red lake and vermilion. The skin has underpainting in a warm, creamy colour in the light areas. [ill.18,19,20]

The final paint layers

The final layers of paint were applied on top of the dead colour and underpainting. Sometimes Vermeer applied the paint thickly to cover, sometimes transparent and thinly for the glazes. Several aspects of his painting technique stand out. The blue sky in the *View of Delft* was painted with long, strong brushstrokes. The grey clouds were painted forcefully. The brush actually lost some hairs which are still visible in the paint.

Vermeer used a very rich palette for the view of the town with its houses and ships. The mixtures of browns and reds, applied with great skill using light but firm strokes, lend a special character to the walls and roofs. The roofs even contain bright yellow and blue. The highlights on the roof tiles for example, are particularly refined.

20 Cross-section of paint from the shadow of the jacket
of *The Girl with a Pearl Earring* (magnification 200x).
Structure of the paint layers:
Paint: ultramarijn, black, organic red, yellow and
brown ochre.
Underpainting: black, brown ochre.
Dead colour: black
Ground: lead white, chalk, red and brown ochre, black.
21 *View of Delft:* firm brushstrokes in the sky.

21

22

23

24

25

The structure of the multicoloured view of the town is highly complex. Vermeer's mastery of his materials is demonstrated by the texture of the bricks and roof tiles. To suggest the texture he sometimes applied the paint as a thick paste (impasto), at other times as a thin, transparent layer over the underpainting. For the texture of other areas the artist mixed coarsely ground lead white with the paint of the underpainting. Elsewhere the surface of the paint has a grainy, almost three-dimensional quality due to the sand mixed into it. The colour intensity of the paint and the light reflected by the sandpaper-like surface result in an extraordinary effect.

Vermeer also mixed sand in with the final layers of paint. The grains are clearly visible, for example in some of the ochre window frames on the roof of the long building to the left behind the city wall.

Many fine hairs from the brush Vermeer used to finish the painted reflections of the buildings in the water remain in the paint. There are also many hairs left on the face of the girl where there are gradual transitions between colours. Painters often used sable brushes to make smooth transitions between areas of paint. [ill.22,23,24,25,26,27]

The Girl with a Pearl Earring shows that the painter applied the paint wet-into-wet. Painters used this technique to blend wet paint directly on the canvas. On the blue turban, the blue fabric is defined by half-round brushstrokes. During painting the details with light and dark strokes of ultramarine were mixed wet-into-wet.

This technique can also be seen in the yellow-green jacket. Vermeer indicated the tiny, yellow light reflections with his characteristic, almost pointillist painting technique. The girl's jacket is painted in such a free style that the nature of the cloth cannot be determined. In his treatise on painting from 1642 Philips Angel stated that the painter should clearly 'distinguish between silk, velvet, wool and worsted, as one rarely sees velvet clothes which appear to have the lustre of velvet, nor can the folds and drapes be seen...'.[17] However, Vermeer decided not to suggest any fabric in particular although the tiny light

22 *View of Delft:* the glass in the window is painted smoothly while the paint used for the window frames and roof is loaded with grains of lead white and sand.

23 *View of Delft:* grainy impasto of the buildings on the left.

24 *View of Delft* (detail): impasto and grainy paint, partly applied wet-into-wet.

25 *View of Delft:* detail of a window, the paint contains sand.

26 *View of Delft:* fragments of stiff brush hairs embedded in the paint of the reflection in the water.

27 *The Girl with a Pearl Earring:* sable hair in the paint between the nose and lips.

26 27

28

reflections, also seen in the shadow below the collar, may suggest a woollen fabric.

The transitions on the cheeks and around the nose, from pink to greenish shadows are soft and smooth. The brushstrokes cannot be seen with the naked eye. Clearly, specific painting techniques were deliberately used to obtain a smooth, flowing effect. This contrasts with the freely painted fabric which has a more solid appearance. Certain parts of the *View of Delft* also suggest rapid brushstrokes. This painting method is somewhat at odds with Angel's ideas. According to him, artists should paint such that '...life can be imitated so closely that it approaches reality, without one ever being aware of the methods the Master used to create it...'.[18]
However, here the methods of the master are clearly visible. This underlines that Vermeer was certainly not a *fijnschilder* (group of painters who painted highly detailed paintings).

The study of the effects and painting techniques used in these two paintings provided much new information and greatly contributed to the understanding of Vermeer's technique.

28 *View of Delft:* boats at the Schiedam Gate, partly painted wet-into-wet.

29 *The Girl with a Pearl Earring:* the blue turban was painted wet-into-wet.

30 *The Girl with a Pearl Earring:* yellow light reflections on the jacket.

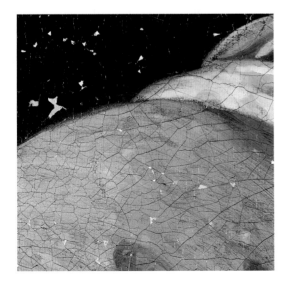

29

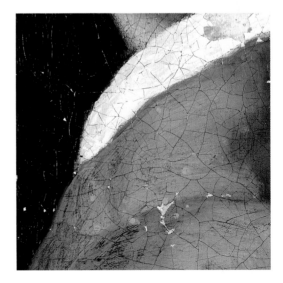

30

Introduction

The recent restorations of the two Vermeers at the Mauritshuis are described in detail to illustrate the restoration history of the paintings and the stages in their treatment.

> Conservation refers to the steps taken to slow down the processes of ageing and decay to ensure the survival of works of art. This includes not only climate control and making sure the objects are stored under optimum conditions but also certain forms of restoration. Restoration refers to the treatment of an art object which may involve some intervention in the structure of the object or work in order to improve its accessibility and aesthetic appeal, or possibly for conservation reasons.

Any conservation activity or restoration should be preceded by a thorough investigation of the materials of the work of art. This will not only enable the conservator to become familiar with the object but also provide an opportunity to identify the problems and suggest a method for their treatment. In addition, information may be obtained which contributes to our understanding of the history of the object.

> Firstly, all aspects of the painting are closely examined with the naked eye and using a stereomicroscope to provide information about the creation of the painting and the effects of ageing. [ill.31]

As much information as possible about the materials, structure and condition of Vermeer's paintings was collected by means of an extensive survey. Information about the history of the paintings and earlier restoration work was also collected, together with the available photographic evidence. Following this stage of the investigations, it became clear what further photographic and scientific investigations would be required.

Tiny paint samples were taken to investigate the structure and composition of the paint layers. These samples are used to make cross-sections of the paint which can be analysed under a microscope. A paint sample is embedded in plastic resin and then ground to reveal the structure of the paint layer. In this way the thickness of the paint and varnish layers and the type and grain size of the pigments can be determined.

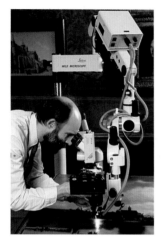

31

31 Restorer Jørgen Wadum examining the *View of Delft*.

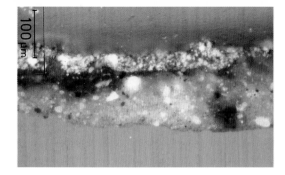

Scientific studies were needed to understand certain phenomena and to solve particular problems associated with the restoration. The painting researcher, Karin Groen, and others worked on this with the Central Research Laboratory for Objects of Art and Science in Amsterdam. The specialists at this institute can analyse the materials used in art objects, in this case pigments and binding media such as resins and linseed oil. They use sophisticated equipment and techniques such as gas chromatography and infrared spectrography. Further investigations and analyses, such as electron microscopy, were carried out at the laboratories of DSM Research in Geleen and the FOM Institute of Atomic and Molecular Physics in Amsterdam. The Scientific Research Department of the National Gallery of Art in Washington also undertook analyses for the Mauritshuis.

32 *View of Delft:* cross-section of the paint of the leaves on a red roof. The blue grains are ultramarine, obtained from a semi-precious stone also known as lapis lazuli.
33 Penetration of the different types of radiation used to investigate paintings.

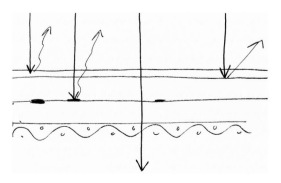

34 Conservator J.C. Traas during the previous restoration in 1960.

34

18

35 After cleaning in 1960.

36 Electron micrograph (SEM) of the wax / resin lining adhesive (DSM).

37 Infrared spectrogram (Central Laboratory) of the lining adhesive. The trough at wavenumber 1387.1 is due to colophony resin and the trough at wavenumber 1174.4 is due to wax.

38 The turban before restoration.

3.1 THE GIRL WITH A PEARL EARRING

Restoration history

The conservation of old paintings often included lining, i.e. a new canvas was stuck to the back of the original support.[19] The adhesive was a mixture of beeswax and resin or a water-based paste (starch). Heated irons where then used to join the canvasses. This treatment not only reinforced the support but also consolidated any loose paint. As far as we were aware, *The Girl with a Pearl Earring* had been lined twice: in 1960 using a wax-resin mixture and in 1882, probably with paste. It is assumed that paste was used because the original canvas has shrunk considerably, which occurs when it is exposed to large amounts of water. Due to the shrinkage there is less space for the paint layer. As a result the paint islands overlap in several areas.

According to a newspaper cutting, the lining in 1882 was carried out in Antwerp by Van der Haeghen.[20] It is likely that the edges by which the canvas was originally stretched were partly cut off for the early lining. The following year the painting was sold at an auction for only 2.30 Dutch guilders.

This indicates that the painting was not greatly appreciated at the time. This is also suggested by the inadequate storage of the painting in the preceding period.[21] The serious loss of paint it had suffered became painfully apparent during the current restoration.

When the painting arrived at the Mauritshuis in 1903 the then director, Mr Bredius, wrote '...[the painting] has many overpaintings which appear to have been applied to hide seriously overcleaned areas of the painting...'.[22] It was only treated in 1915. It was 'Cleaned, regenerated and varnished by D. de Wild', who was the in-house restorer of the Mauritshuis, at a cost of five guilders.[23] De Wild noted '...only the upper layer of varnish was regenerated; the lower layers cannot be regenerated, otherwise the retouches in the varnish would dissolve and they would have to be removed and redone completely.'[24] The entry for 1922 once again notes 'Varnish restored by D. de Wild.'[25]

In 1960 *The Girl with a Pearl Earring* was lined with a wax-resin mixture onto a fine linen cloth with a close weave. The original canvas was thereby fully impregnated by the wax-resin mixture. The remaining tacking edges were folded outward, thus the painting is now larger than it used to be.

The treatment was summarised at the time as 'Lined, varnish removed and some retouches improved by J.C. Traas.'[26]

35

The photographs from 1960 indicate that only about 90% of the old retouches were removed. It appears that Mr Traas did not remove the old retouches on the eye but only touched them up again. [ill.35]

Condition of the painting in spring 1994

The Girl with a Pearl Earring was in a relatively good state of conservation. There were no imminent threats to the material condition of the painting. The wax-resin lining was still in an excellent condition and there was no loose paint.

A tiny sample of the wax-resin mixture was enlarged under an electron microscope. The extent of ageing can be roughly determined from the surface. The surface is not broken up and is relatively smooth. The wax-resin on the painting still feels relatively soft. [ill.36]
The molecular composition of substances can be analysed by infrared spectrography. This graph indicates the components of the wax-resin mixture. The composition of the mixture can be determined by comparison with analyses of known substances. The ratio of this mixture was estimated at one part of wax to one part of resin.[27] [ill.37]

However, from an aesthetic point of view, the painting was not in good condition. The varnish had yellowed considerably and the old retouches had discoloured to such an extent that they looked like dark shadows. The retouches were particularly noticeable in the blue headband, the background and the shadows of the figure.

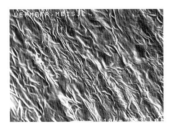

36

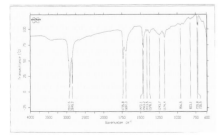

37

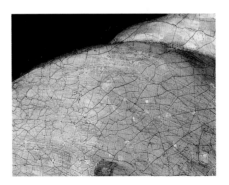

39

40

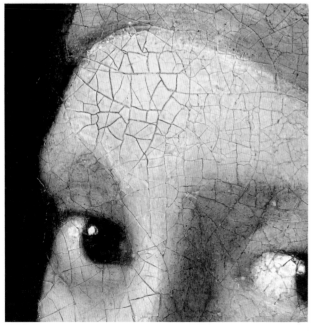

41

39 Photograph taken under ultraviolet light. The dark areas are retouches.

40 X-ray.

41 Forehead of the girl with deliberately darkened craquelure.

42 Detail of the lips

42

When a painting is exposed to ultraviolet light, which is invisible to the naked eye, it will fluoresce. Each substance fluoresces differently. UV light can be used to reveal details on the surface of the painting. For example, old varnish often has a greenish fluorescence but later overpainting and retouches applied onto the original paint or onto the varnish interfere with the fluorescence and appear as dark areas. [ill.38,39]

The oil paint shows age-cracking. Apart from a network of fine cracks there also appear to be wider and darker cracks, particularly on the left side of the face. Some of these were found to have been deliberately darkened during an earlier restoration while others were filled with brown discoloured wax and old varnish.

> Some of the cracks on the forehead and the cheek of the face were deliberately darkened which made the painting look even older. [ill.41]

Paint has been lost from almost all areas of the painting. The largest lacunae are at the bottom and on the face. This is primarily due to storage under poor conditions in a particularly poor climate and due to rough handling.

> X-rays are highly absorbed by paint layers with pigments containing lead and mercury. These materials show up lighter on X-ray photographs. The first coating applied to the canvas by the painter, the ground, contains lead white. The penetration of the ground between the threads of the canvas clearly reveals the pattern of the woven linen on the X-ray photograph. From the undulations between the stretching points we can examine the way the painting was stretched.
> The lightest parts of the painting, and the lit parts of the face contain large amounts of lead white. These areas show up best on the X-ray photograph. The lacunae in the painting show up as small black spots. As the paint and ground are missing in these areas, the X-rays are not absorbed and so they show up black on the film. [ill.40]

> The varnish, pigmented with a little black, had yellowed considerably due to ageing. In some areas it had broken up which scatters incident light and produces an unfortunate effect. [ill.42,44]

43 Craquelure patterns on *The Girl with a Pearl Earring.*
A: cob-web craquelure occurs when a single point is subjected to exessive stress. B: fine cracks appear immediately after application of the ground layer. These work through the ground up to the surface. C: age cracking occurs when the paint film becomes brittle and cracks. D: the craquelure in these areas is the result of the wedges (the small pieces of wood used to tighten the stretcher) being hit too vigorously. E: painted craquelure on the girl's forehead and cheek.
44 Detail of photo 42.

44

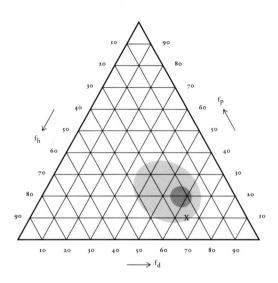

45

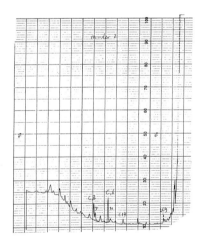

46

The 1994 restoration

The purpose of the restoration was defined by the museum restorers and conservators after consulting the international support committee. The yellowed varnish would have to be removed and the discoloured retouches and poor fillings would also be removed. The painting would then be sparingly retouched with stable materials and revarnished.

Analysis of the varnish revealed that it was almost pure dammar, a natural resin. Some black pigment had been added to it to change its hue. The varnish was carefully removed using cotton swabs and a solvent mixture which dissolved the varnish without affecting the paint.

> The forces between the molecules of a solvent, which can be expressed by three parameters, determine its dissolving power. A simple way to present this information is in the form of a graph, a Teas diagram. The solubility of materials such as dried resins and oils, as determined in experiments, can also be expressed in this diagram.[28] [ill.45]
> This diagram (which shows the solubility of oil paint [dark grey] and natural resins [light grey]) can be used to determine fairly reliably those solvent mixtures which will dissolve the resin without affecting the oil paint. The mixture used to clean The Girl with a Pearl Earring is indicated by a cross.

Some retouches were removed together with the varnish while others were more difficult to dissolve. The tenacious retouches were first thinned by scraping with a surgical scalpel, leaving only a thin residue. Then they could be removed generally by undercutting, i.e. the layer of varnish below the hard retouches is dissolved with solvent, thus releasing them from the outer edges inward.

> The binding medium of the old, insoluble retouches was analysed by gas chromatography. The analysis indicated components typical of old, dried linseed oil. This explained why it was so difficult to remove the retouches with the selected solvent. [ill.46]

Once all the material applied to the original painting had been removed Vermeer's clear, fresh and extremely delicate use of colour were revealed.

47

Certain details, characteristic of Vermeer's technique which – sometimes comes close to pointillism – that had been hidden for years were also revealed. The small light reflection near the left corner of her mouth is an example of this. This highlight consists of two small pale pink spots of paint on top of each other. Vermeer painted a similar highlight on the lips of *The Girl with a Red Hat* in Washington.[29]

48

49

47 Varnish being removed with a cotton swab and solvent.

48 The cheek of the girl, largely cleaned. On the left the yellowed and pigmented varnish is still visible. On the right this intrusive layer has been removed.

49 Mouth of the girl, after cleaning.

50 Cross-section through the painting with excess filler and retouches. *6 retouch; 5 filling; 4 varnish; 3 paint layer; 2 ground; 1 canvas*

51 Cross-section through the painting with the loose paint fragment.

52 Excess filler is removed with a scalpel.

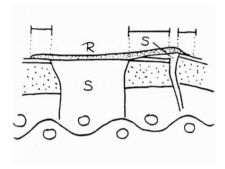

50

24   51

52

Once the painting was cleaned everybody was puzzled by why so many retouches had been made. It appeared that after an earlier restoration, excess filler had been left on top of the paint. The restorer had had to retouch this as well as the actual fillings.

> There was a lot of old and excess filler on the painting. Two generations of fillings were discernable: from 1882 and from the most recent treatment in 1960. Much of the recent filler, a mixture of chalk and glue, was on top of the original, intact paint. As the paint surface is not quite flat, most of the white material was concentrated along the raised edges of the paint islands. As the previous restorer had not carefully removed this material at the time, it had been left in place and hardened. He had then retouched the white areas. [ill.50]

However, it was not just excess filler on the painting which was hidden by the old retouches. From the start of the investigations the restorers had wondered what caused some inexplicable white specks on the X-ray photograph. These occurred in areas where the painting was unlikely to contain concentrations of lead white. After cleaning it was revealed that the white dots on the photograph were flakes of original paint which had stuck to other parts of the painting. These paint fragments were now upside down, with the light ground facing up. It is most likely that this occurred in 1882 when the adhesion of the paint was apparently very poor.

> The fragments of paint which came loose and stuck to other parts of the painting had been pressed into the surface of the paint during lining. At the end of the 19th century heavy, hot irons were used for lining. The pressure and heat of the irons could easily distort the paint layer. [ill.51]

For many decades the pearl had three light reflections. There is a large, teardrop-shaped highlight on the left of the pearl. This reflection is caused by the light which hits the face from the top left. At the bottom, the shape of the pearl is defined in white-grey: the reflection of the white collar of the girl's blouse. This reflection is half as bright as the large highlight. These effects were discussed in detail in 17th century treatises on painting.
For example, according to Samuel van Hoogstraeten 'Shine is

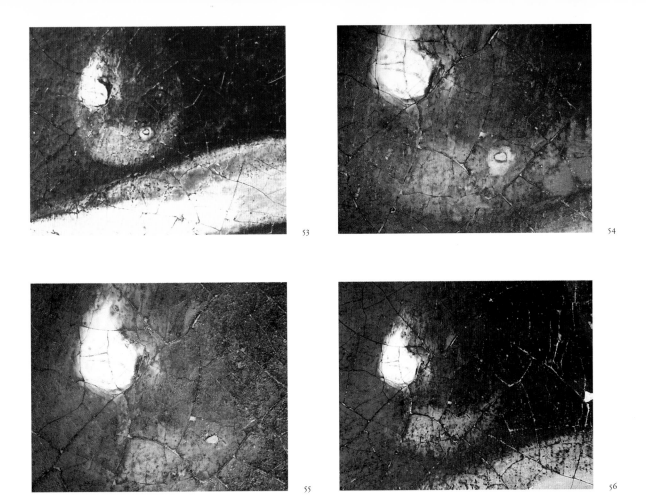

53   The pearl in 1904.

54   The pearl before cleaning.

55   The pearl after removal of the excess filler.

56   The pearl after removal of the small flake of paint on the pearl.

essentially the reflection of the light of all illuminated objects, but in art we only use the term reflection or shine for the second light in the shadow'.[30] The second light reflection on the pearl contained another small, bright highlight which was not actually part of the original painting. This 'reflection' turned out to be no more than a flake of paint surrounded by filler which must have accidentally stuck to this spot during an earlier restoration.

This misleading 'highlight' was removed. Although the paint surface of the pearl is now slightly deformed and worn, this more closely reflects the original intention of the artist.

> Vermeer used accents in the impasto to render the texture of the yellow turban. The highlights in the eyes and on the pearl and the tiny yellow dots on the jacket are also relatively thickly applied. These touches were largely flattened by the lining in the past. Furthermore, any flaws, such as loose paint flakes and filler residues on the painting at the time of the lining, were pressed into the original paint layer. The once lively surface texture was largely lost as a result of the lining. [ill.57,58]

Once the painting had been cleaned the next stage of the restoration could commence. Small lacunae were filled with a mixture of chalk and animal glue. Damaged old fillings were carefully repaired. The structure of the fillings should precisely match that of the surrounding paint, otherwise the retouches would stand out, even if they were done in the right colour.

57

58

59

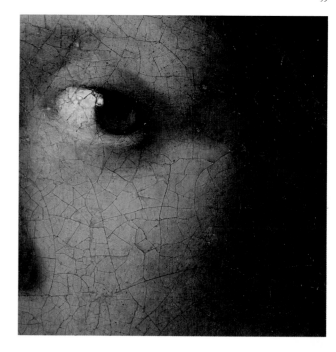

26

57 Paintings were lined and flattened with hot irons.

58 Photograph of the collar in raking light.

59 *The Girl with a Pearl Earring* before the 1994 restoration.

60 Cheek, after cleaning, before the application of the new filling.

61 The retouch on the cheek of the girl is first underpainted in the shades used by Vermeer.

62 The painting with the new fillings and isolating varnish.

After removing the excess filler and the loose paint fragments, more of Vermeer's original paint was revealed. New fillings were limited to the lacunae visible in the X-ray photograph. [ill.62]

The painting was then given a thin coat of isolating varnish. This saturates the colours so that they are clearly visible during the retouching and also forms a buffer between the original and the retouches. The varnish was based on dammar resin. The components and behaviour of this natural resin are well known. We know how this material ages and that it remains relatively soluble so that it can be removed without damage to the paint.

62

60

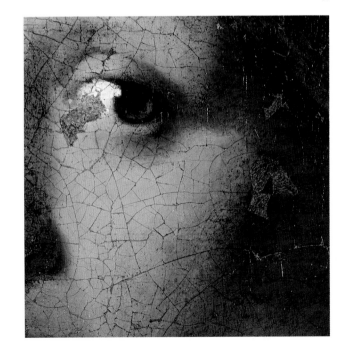

61

27

The retouches were made by underpainting in watercolour with a transparent glaze of a synthetic resin ground with dry pigment. Unlike the old oil paint retouches, the composition of these paints is such that they will show little or no discolouration in future. The watercolour paint and pigments are light-fast and the binding medium, a synthetic resin, is also extremely stable.[31]

One of the most important aspects of restorations is that they should be reversible. When necessary, it should be possible to remove all the materials applied to a work of art without detriment to the original. The varnish and the retouching materials used on *The Girl with a Pearl Earring* all meet this criterion.

> Retouching was carried out in two stages. The aim was to take the same approach that Vermeer used. First, the basic colours were applied in watercolour to the lacunae. The transparent finishing layers, the glazes, and the final accents were then applied in synthetic resin mixed with dry pigment. In this way the depth of colour could be imitated. [ill.61]

Finally a colourless varnish was applied to obtain a uniform gloss and to protect the surface of the painting and the new retouches. Dammar resin was selected, with the addition of a stabiliser to retard ageing and the attendant yellowing.[32]

This restoration has revitalised the aesthetic aspects of *The Girl with a Pearl Earring*. The colour balance which was distorted by the yellowed varnish has been corrected. The distracting discoloured retouches and overpainting have been removed. This has restored the masterly three-dimensional effect of the painting. The subtle skin tones, brilliant eyes and light reflections on the lips are once again revealed in their full glory.

63 Restorer Nicola Costaras retouching.

64 The painting after restoration.

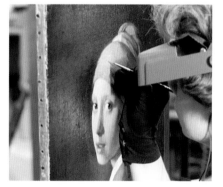

63

28

Restoration history

The *View of Delft* has been restored a number of times since it was acquired by the Mauritshuis in 1822. Nothing is known about any restorations before this time. In 1841 the painting was 'washed and varnished twice' by the restorer, N. Hopman.[33]

In 1875, over thirty years later '...the canvas of the painting was lined by Mr W.A. Hopman...'.[34] As there is no further documentation on this treatment we do not know exactly what materials he used and how the lining was carried out. It is also not specified whether or not the painting was cleaned although it seems likely that it was.

Recent analysis of the composition of the lining adhesive revealed that it is a wax/resin mixture. The infrared spectrogram gives the components of the sample. The wax/resin ratio is probably 3 : 7. This lining adhesive is much harder than the mixture used to line the Girl with a Pearl Earring.[35] [ill.65,66]

65   *The View of Delft*, c. 1886.

65

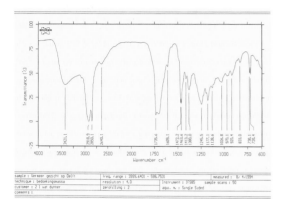

66

67

66 Electron micrograph (SEM) of the wax/resin lining
adhesive (DSM).

67 Infrared spectrogram of the lining adhesive (Central
Laboratory).

68 X-ray (detail), hole in the sky.

69 Detail: hole in the sky.

The wax/resin mixture is brittle but still provides good adhesion. The surface of the sample was photographed with an electron microscope.

The following year the painting was damaged. While work was in progress in the room, a curtain rod fell down and made a hole in the centre of the painting.[36] The painting was restored by W.A. Hopman.[37]

> The hole in the painting is clearly visible on the X-ray. After removal of the varnish and retouches, the extent of the damage was found to correspond with the X-ray. The 1876 repair is visible on the back of the painting. The hole was repaired with a thin layer of filler. [ill.68,69]

In 1956 J.C. Traas, then the Mauritshuis restorer, carried out another restoration of the painting. According to the annual reports, this amounted to little more than removing the old varnish.

> According to the 1957 annual report, the old coats of varnish were removed in 1956 '...without significant risk... The painting was found to be in an almost incredibly good condition, there was no need for anything other than the removal of several coats of old varnish and there was no need for any restoration, i.e. retouching old damage or worn areas, with the exception of one area of less than one square centimetre in the clouds.'[38] However, photographs of this restoration show that the extent of the intervention was greatly understated. The curtain rod had made a hole of about three square centimetres and considerable retouching had been applied to other areas. [ill.70]

31

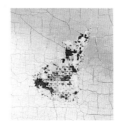

68

69

Vermeer had originally painted a man in the foreground, on the bank
of the Delftse Schie to the right of the two women. However, he then
overpainted this figure. Such changes by an artist are sometimes
referred to by the Italian word 'pentimento'. The painting includes a
number of pentimenti which can be revealed by infrared
reflectography. Such changes have also been found in other paintings
by Vermeer.[39]

Infrared radiation can penetrate paint layers to some extent. The
reflected radiation can then be recorded on photographic film.
Alternatively, an infrared-sensitive video camera can be used to study
small areas of paintings. The details are then displayed on a monitor.
This information can then be recorded photographically or digitally
stored and processed. This method is much more sensitive than infrared
photography and is known as infrared reflectography.[40] This technique
not only reveals underdrawing in black but also some changes and
alterations in the deeper paint layers which are normally invisible.
Several pentimenti are visible on these infrared reflectograms, here
shown as a montage of photographs of images displayed on the
monitor. For example, the boats Vermeer painted on the right, at the
Rotterdam Gate, were originally smaller. He extended their sterns to
the left and they now cover part of the underpainting of the gate which
was done at an earlier stage. On the painting these elements are now
just discernible through the dark paint of the boats. [ill.71]

The pentimento of a man at the waterside, in the foreground, was
revealed during restoration in 1956. Older photographs, from before
1956, show a dark, retouched area slightly larger than the overpainted
figure. The conservator, Mr Traas, removed the retouches which partly
revealed the man. This happened when the old varnish was removed
which also removed some of the old retouches. He then correctly
retouched the painting to cover the man in accordance with Vermeer's
intention.[41] Unfortunately there is no written information about the
figure. The only information is provided by some photographs from the
period. [ill.72,73]

70

71

32

After completion of the restoration the press reported '...This painting had long been disfigured by a yellow-brown varnish. This dirt was carefully removed to reveal the bright colours beneath'. And '...As a result of the work of the government restorer, Mr J Traas, we can now enjoy the vivid colours of Vermeer's painting style'.[42] This would not lead one to suspect that Traas actually used a tinted, light-yellow varnish in some areas to reduce the brilliance of the painting in those areas.[43]

In the past, when 'old masters' lost their 'golden glow' after removal of the varnish, they were often considered to be too bright. For this reason restorers used to give the paintings a 'gallery tone' by using yellow or pigmented varnish. It was assumed, wrongly, that the old varnish was part of the 'patina'. However, nowadays the patina only refers to aging of the original materials, such as the craquelure, fading of certain pigments and the ageing, e.g. increasing transparency, of the binding medium. These coloured varnishes detracted greatly from the original intentions of the artists.[44]

As the coloured varnish coats had also greatly yellowed after as little as 25 years, their composition was investigated even in the 1980s.

72

73

74

72 The pentimento during the 1956 restoration.
73 Detail of the pentimento in raking light, before the 1994 restoration.
74 The pentimento during the 1994 restoration.

In 1982 samples of the varnish were taken from the edges of the *View of Delft*. Further investigations indicated that the varnish contained shellac. Shellac, obtained from a secretion of the lac insect, is a very brittle material which would never be used as a varnish for paintings in its pure state. When it ages shellac becomes so insoluble that aggressive solvents have to be used to remove the varnish which might also affect the paint film. Therefore, if the varnish contained shellac it would be best to remove it as soon as possible.

There was some doubt as to whether the paint still adhered sufficiently to the support. As early as 1984 external advice suggested that some of the paint islands might become detached from the support.[45] It was therefore decided that the varnish should be removed in order to assess the condition of the paint layers. Any loose paint would then be secured.

Condition of the painting in spring 1994

Generally speaking, the *View of Delft* was in a good condition. However, to guarantee its conservation the condition of the paint adhesion would have to be investigated. This required the removal of the varnish. Furthermore, the appearance of the painting was disfigured by the coloured and greatly darkened coats of varnish which were also irregular and uneven.

New varnish samples were taken, further from the edges. Unlike the earlier analyses, this time no shellac was found. It may be that the earlier analyses were affected by shellac residue from the picture frame. This eliminated any fears about the poor solubility of the material. However, the scientific analysis revealed that the varnish used in 1956 consisted of colophony, a natural resin. This is known to yellow relatively quickly. It was also found that a small quantity of oil had been mixed into the colophony of one of the varnish coats.[46] This mixture aroused further concern about the solubility of the varnish.

Colophony is a resin which was often used in the lining adhesive for wax/resin linings. Sometimes small quantities of colophony were added to the varnish to increase its gloss and hardness. However, if a coat of pure colophony is used as a varnish it will be very shiny and rapidly embrittle and yellow. This is exactly what had happened to the *View of Delft*.

75 Detail of the sky in raking light, before the 1994 restoration.

34

75

Raking light reveals how uneven the surface of the paint is. The paint islands in the sky have suffered most from cupping, they are level in the centre but their edges have curled up. This cupping is most prevalent in areas where Vermeer mixed a lot of lead white into his paint.

> View of Delft: before removal of the varnish:
> Due to the coloured and yellowed varnish, the clouds in the sky appeared to be browner than they are. The varnish had collected in the bottom of the paint islands. This led to increased local yellowing which made the varnish look blotchy. [ill.76]

> The blue is surprisingly clear. It appears that the ultramarine has not discoloured as it has in some paintings by Vermeer's contemporaries. Such discolouration is sometimes referred to as 'ultramarine disease'. [ill.77]

76

77

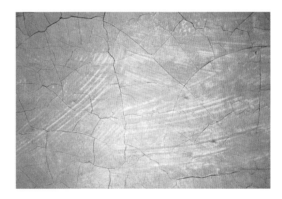

78

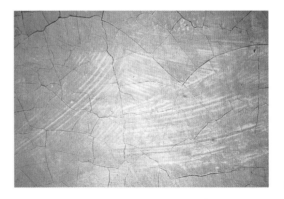

79

76 Detail of the sky before removing the varnish.

77 Detail of the sky after removing the varnish.

78 Detail of the sky after removing the varnish showing retouches from 1956.

79 Detail of the sky fully cleaned.

35

The corners had broken off the raised edges of the paint islands, probably due to the lining in 1875. However, these paint fragments were preserved and are now embedded in the wax/resin mixture by which the whole painting is impregnated.

Many small fragments of paint and ground are missing from the buildings of the town. The linen is visible through these lacunae which were not filled during earlier restorations. Sometime in the past, the adhesion between the paint layers in the dark reflection of the Schiedam Gate was lost and part of the topmost paint layer is now missing in this area.[47]

The retouches made in 1956 are more extensive than suggested by the description in the 1957 annual report and old photographs. Although they are thin they are also discoloured. They have also been applied to many areas of the painting other than the area where the canvas was penetrated by the curtain rod. Not only the reflection of the Schiedam Gate in the water but also the overpainted man in the foreground were retouched. At that time much of the craquelure and minor damage to the thinly painted sky were also covered up. Even thin, but undamaged, brushstrokes in blue were retouched by the restorer, as if he wanted to improve on Vermeer's technique. [ill.10]

80 The 1956 retouches are indicated on the overlay.

80

81

81 Removing the varnish.

Unlike the varnish of *The Girl with a Pearl Earring,*
which was removed completely, the varnish on the *View
of Delft* was only reduced to a thin layer.

The 1994 restoration

The treatment of the *View of Delft* was primarily aimed at removing the discoloured varnish and to check the adhesion of the paint. The intention was also to return the painting to its original appearance. While the varnish was being removed, it was checked whether the adhesion of the edges of the paint islands was sufficient. The danger of cupping is that the raised edges of the paint lift to such an extent that they become separated from the support and flakes of paint become detached. A thorough assessment of the paint layer indicated that the adhesion of the paint was still good. Despite the earlier concern, there was no need to secure any of the paint. Apparently, the lining adhesive used in 1875 had effectively penetrated the structure of the painting and had not lost any of its adhesion.

The removal of the varnish was complicated as there were several layers of varnish and retouches and because a thin layer of varnish had to be preserved.[48] The surface of the paint was also very irregular. At times, the varnish had to be removed with cotton swabs and solvent one island at a time, and mostly under a stereomicroscope.
All the old retouches were removed at the same time, including those on the pentimento of the man in the foreground. It soon became clear that this figure is now more visible because Vermeer's retouch has become more transparent and because someone removed part of this retouch in the past. The many traces left by a knife or scalpel suggested that it was almost as if someone had tried to expose the man.
Unfortunately, after removing the major retouches to the right of this pentimento, it was found that the upper layer of paint had suffered far more damage than was expected. The right-hand part of the dark reflection of the Schiedam Gate and the light water to the right of this, in particular, have suffered serious and inexplicable damage. The older retouches and photographs from 1956 suggest that this damage had already occurred by then.
After the application of isolating varnish these areas were again retouched. The man was overpainted in the spirit of Vermeer. Again, watercolour was used for the underpainting and synthetic resin mixed with dry pigment was used for the glazes.[49]

Finally, the *View of Delft* was given a thin coat of colourless dammar varnish with the addition of a stabiliser. This varnish imparts an even gloss to the painting.

The condition of the *View of Delft* was assessed in detail during these restoration activities. Previous concerns about the adhesion of the

37

82

83

38

84

85

Various stages in the removal of the varnish and
retouches from the same area.

82 Before removing the varnish.

83 Removing the varnish. Varnish removal is irregular,
possibly due to linseed oil on the retouches or in the
varnish layers.

84 The old retouches are revealed.

85 The retouches have been removed.

86 Detail of the view of the town, before restoration.

87 Detail of the view of the town, after restoration.

86

87

paint to the support appeared to be unfounded. The removal of the deliberately coloured and now yellowed varnish layers applied in the past, spectacularly revealed Vermeer's sparkling palette. The investigation of the technical aspects of the painting produced much new information which will be of great value for further comparative studies of Vermeer's oeuvre.

88 After making the new fillings but before retouching. The new retouches were largely limited to the hole in the sky, Vermeer's pentimento of the man and the worn reflection of the Schiedam Gate.

89 Restorer Luuk Struick van der Loeff during retouching.

90 *The View of Delft* after restoration.

88

89

4. Afterword

In 1642 Philips Angel wrote that no painting '...is assured of immortality: they are affected by change, nothing remains unchanged other than God who is eternal and everlasting; thus paintings may last a few hundred years, which is enough ...'.[50]
Clearly, the natural ageing of the materials used in the paintings cannot be halted. However, the ageing processes can be slowed down by ensuring that the paintings are kept in the best possible conditions and by caring for them. It is to be hoped that as a result of the conservation and restoration of *The Girl with a Pearl Earring* and the *View of Delft* we will be able to enjoy them for longer than the 'few hundred years' assumed by Angel.

Through the public nature of the restoration of both paintings and the publication of the results of the investigations, we hope that museum visitors are now more aware of an important aspect of museum work which is normally carried out behind the scenes.

91 The public restoration studio

91

43

Notes

1. Johannes Vermeer

1. Montias, 1993.

2. *The Little Street* (canvas, 54.3 x 44 cm), c. 1657-1658.

3. Previously it was assumed that the clock showed ten past seven. However, in the 17th century these clocks only had a single hand. This information was provided by Wim Weve.

4. Blankert, 1992, p. 218: M. Proust, 1921, *Correspondence générale*, 'Lettres à J.L. Vaudoyer', Paris, 1921.

5. Blankert, 1992, p. 217: M. du Camp, *En Hollande, Lettres à un ami*, 1859.

6. *Portrait of a Young Woman* (canvas, 44.5 x 40 cm), Metropolitan Museum of Art, c. 1666-1667.

2. Vermeer's Painting Techniques

7. Montias, 1993, doc. 364, p. 387.

8. The Allegory of Painting (canvas, 119 x 100 cm), c. 1666-1667, Kunsthistorisches Museum; Allegory of the Faith (canvas, 114.3 x 88.7 cm), c. 1671-1674, Metropolitan Museum of Art.

9. *The Girl with a Red Hat* (panel, 23 x 18 cm), c. 1666-1667; *Young Girl with a Flute* (panel, 20 x 18 cm), c. 1666-1667.

10. Montias, doc. 364, p. 387.

11. Another painting by Vermeer in the Mauritshuis, *Diana and her Companions*, was probably trimmed on the right. The current dimensions of the painting are 97.5 x 105.5 cm. If this is extended on the right by about 15 cm to include the missing area affected by cusping, the size of the painting would be similar to that of the *View of Delft*.

12. Bruyn, 1979; Miedema, 1981; Wadum, 1988; Van de Wetering, 1986.

13. Most of the landscapes in the Mauritshuis were painted on canvasses with a height to width ratio of 1:1.40. Most of the genre paintings have a ratio of 1:1.30. On average, portraits have a ratio of 1:1.20 and tend to be rather square.

14. Cross-sections of the grounds of both paintings were studied by H. Kühn in 1966 (see Kühn, 1968) and by K. Groen in 1994. Both investigations indicated the same pigments.

15. Van de Graaf, 1958, p. 16a.

16. See note 8.

17. Angel, 1642, p. 55; Sluijter, 1993.

18. Angel, 1642, p. 53.

3.1 Girl with a Pearl Earring

19. (This endnote refers to some terminological confusion in Dutch. It is not relevant in English.)

20. According to the newspaper article about the new addition to the collection '...Nothing is known about this painting other than that it was lined by Van der Haeghen in Antwerp...'. Nieuwe Courant, 2-3-1903.

21. Nieuwe Courant, 1903: 'When it was acquired by Mr Des Tombes [1881] it was in a sorry state of neglect.'

22. Mauritshuis archives, 1903 Inventory records.

23. Claim by W. de Wild in 1915. The restoration was carried out at his studio at the Buys Ballotstraat 29, The Hague. Mauritshuis archives. Regeneration was the softening of brittle and clouded varnish with alcohol vapour and often by the application of copaiba balsam. This method is no longer used. See: Schmitt, 1990.

24. Documentation of the restoration studio of the Mauritshuis (B), cor. nos. 218, 225 and 1916 no. 83.

25. Index of the Annual Reports of the Mauritshuis, p. 40.

26. Index of the Annual Reports of the Mauritshuis.

27. The wax-resin ratio could not be accurately determined, the estimate of 1:1 was based on other investigations. These analyses were carried out by K. Groen on 8-4-1994.

28. Banik & Krist, 1984.

29. See note 9.

30. Hoogstraeten, 1678, p. 262.

31. Mowilith-20, a polyvinylacetate.

32. Tinuvin 292 (Ciba-Geigy), a Hindered Amine Stabiliser (HALS). See: De la Rie and McGlinchey, 1990, p. 160.

3.2 View of Delft

33. Mauritshuis archives, letter no. 639. In 1871, W.A. Hopman, also a restorer defined 'washing' as: cleaning the surface with 'old white Marseille soap'. The painting probably had to be varnished twice because the water must have affected the old varnish and turned it white. See: von Pettenkofer, ed. 1871, p. 49.

34. Mauritshuis annual report 1875, p. 7. He used canvas of herringbone twill weave. It is likely that the strainer or stretcher was replaced by the present one at the same time.

35. Analysis by K. Groen.

36. Mr De Jonge, then director of the Mauritshuis, reported this incident to the Minister by letter on 13 April 1876: '[a workman who] ...only had to replace a worn curtain cord by a new one was inexplicably clumsy and while pulling up a curtain he pulled a frame on the window out of its supports, this frame then fell down and hit painting no. 72 by Johannes Vermeer and caused damage to the sky on this painting which penetrated to the canvas. None of the guards could prevent this happening because it occurred so quickly and unexpectedly. The deputy director and the supervisor Mr Sardijn were close by but only the workman was at fault and I removed him from the building forthwith. In my

view, the reputation of the above painting would be greatly affected if this accident was made public. Therefore, I ask your Excellency's permission for the immediate lining of the painting by Mr Hopman without reference to anyone other than the head of the VIth department [Victor de Stuers]…'. Mauritshuis archives, letter no. 28. This matter was covered up and the restoration is not mentioned in the 1876 annual report.

37. 'The painting can be lined and repaired by Mr Hopman. The costs should be borne by J. Outze, the wallpaper hanger', Documentation of the restoration studio of the Mauritshuis, letter no. 29, April 1876.

38. Mauritshuis annual report 1957, p. 127.

39. In the left foreground of the painting *Young Woman with a Water Jug* (canvas, 45.7 x 40.6 cm), c. 1664-1665, now in the Metropolitan Museum of Art, New York, Vermeer originally included a chair with lion heads. Later he overpainted it. He also painted a lute on a chair in the right foreground of the *Woman with a Pearl Necklace* (canvas, 51.2 x 45.2 cm), c. 1664, Gemäldegalerie, Berlin. Again he removed it at a later stage. See: Wheelock, 1987.

40. This technique was developed by J.R.J. Van Asperen de Boer. See: Van Asperen de Boer, 1970.

41. Martin, 1916-1917, p. 33-41.

42. Haagsche Courant, 3-7-1956.

43. Verbal communication from Mr P.N.H. Domela Nieuwenhuis, deputy scientific officer of the museum during the restoration.

44. Ruhemann, 1968; Brachert, 1985; Hedley, 1993.

45. Mauritshuis archives, letter no. 284 of 6-4-1984.

46. These analyses were carried out by the Scientific Department of the National Gallery in Washington.

47. From the survey it appears that this also affects other paintings by Vermeer.

48. There is no visible discolouration as a result.

49. See note 31.

50. Angel, 1642, p. 25.

Bibliography

Angel 1642: P. Angel, *Lof der Schilder-Konst*, Leiden 1642 (facsimile, Davaco publ. 1969)

Van Asperen de Boer 1970: J.R.J. van Asperen de Boer, *Infrared Reflectography. A Contribution to the Examination of Earlier European Paintings*, Amsterdam 1970

Banik & Krist 1984: G. Banik & G. Krist, *Lösungsmittel in der Restaurierung*, ICCROM, Wien 1984

Blankert 1992: A. Blankert, J.M. Montias & G. Aillaud, *Vermeer*, Amsterdam 1992

Brachert 1985: T. Brachert, *Patina. Von Nutzen und Nachteil der Restaurierung*, München 1985

Bruyn 1979: J. Bruyn, 'Een onderzoek naar 17de-eeuwse schilderijformaten, voornamelijk in Noord-Nederland', *Oud Holland* (1979) 93, p. 96-115

Van de Graaf 1958: J.A. van de Graaf, *Het De Mayerne manuscript als bron voor de schildertechniek van de barok*, Mijdrecht 1958

Hedley 1993: G. Hedley, *Measured Opinions. Collected papers on the conservation of paintings*, [ed. C. Villers] UKIC, London 1993

Hoogstraeten 1678: S. van Hoogstraeten, *Inleyding tot de hooge schoole der Schilderkonst...*, Rotterdam 1678 (facsimile, Davaco publ. 1969)

Kühn 1968: H. Kühn, 'A Study of the Pigments and the Grounds Used by Jan Vermeer', *Report and Studies in the History of Art 1968*, National Gallery of Art, Washington 1968, p. 155-202

Van Mander ed 1973: Karel van Mander, *Den grondt der edel vrij schilder-const*, ed., translated and annotated by H. Miedema, Parts I en II, Utrecht 1973

Martin 1916-17: W. Martin, 'Over conserveeren en restaureren van oude schilderijen, I-IV', *Oude Kunst*, (1916-17), p. 10-17, 33-41, 65-74, 359-365

Miedema 1981: H. Miedema, 'Verder onderzoek naar zeventiende-eeuwse schilderijformaten in Noord-Holland', *Oud Holland* (1981) 95, p. 31-49

Montias 1993: J.M. Montias, *Vermeer en zijn milieu*, Baarn 1993

Von Pettenkofer ed. 1871: M. von Pettenkofer, *Over Olieverven en het*

Conserveeren van Schilderijen door de regeneratie-Behandeling, ed., translated and annotated by W.A. Hopman, Amsterdam 1871

De la Rie & McGlinchey 1990: R. de la Rie & C.W. McGlinchey, 'The effect of a Hindered Amine Light Stabilizer on the Aging of Dammar and Mastic Varnish in an Environment Free of Ultraviolet Light', in: *Cleaning, Retouching and Coatings*, (J.S. Mills & P. Smith eds.), Preprints of the IIC Brussels Congress London 1990

Ruhemann 1968: H. Ruhemann, *The Cleaning of Paintings. Problems & Potentialities*, London 1968

Sluijter 1993: E.J. Sluijter, *De lof der schilderkunst. Over schilderijen van Gerrit Dou en een traktaat van Philips Angel uit 1642*, Zeven Provinciën Reeks (7), Hilversum 1993

Schuitt 1990, S. Schmitt, 'Das Pettenkofersche Regenerationsverfahren – Eine Studie zur Geschichte einer Methode und ihren Auswirkungen', *Zeitschrift für Kunsttechnologie und Konservierung* (1990) 1, p. 30-76

Wadum 1988: J. Wadum, 'The Winter Room at Rosenborg Castle: A Unique Survival of Antwerp Mass-Production', *Apollo*, (1988) vol. CXXVIII (318), p. 82-87

Van de Wetering 1986: E. van de Wetering, *Studies in the workshop practice of the early Rembrandt*, thesis, Amsterdam 1986

Wheelock & Kaldenbach 1982: A.K. Wheelock Jr. & C.J. Kaldenbach, 'Vermeer's View of Delft and his Vision of Reality', *Artibus et historiae*, (1982) 6, p. 9-35

Wheelock 1987: A.K. Wheelock Jr., 'Pentimenti in Vermeer's Paintings: Changes in Style and Meaning', in: 'Holländische Genremalerei in 17.Jahrhundert, Symposium Berlin 1984', *Jahrbuch Preußischer Kulturbesitz* (1987) 4, pp. 385-412

Further Reading

D. Arasse, *Vermeer. Faith in Painting,* Princeton 1994

K. Beltinger, 'Craquelé op schilderijen', *kM, vakinformatie voor beeldende kunstenaars en restauratoren,* (1993) 8, p.13-18

H. Brammer, 'Durch Restaurierungsmassnahmen beschädigte Bilder', *Zeitschrift für Kunsttechnologie und Konservierung* (1987) 1, p. 95-104

S. Bucklow, 'The Effect of Craquelure. Upon the Perception of the Pictorial Image', *Zeitschrift für Kunsttechnologie und Konservierung* (1994) 8, p. 104-111

A. Clydesdale, *Chemicals in Conservation: A Guide to Possible Hazards and Safe Use,* Conservation Bureau, SSCR, Edinburgh 1982

R.L. Feller, N. Stolow & E.H. Jones, *On Picture Varnishes and their Solvents,* National Gallery of Art, Washington 1985

R.L. Feller, *Artists' Pigments. A Handbook of their History and Characteristics,* National Gallery of Art, Washington, D.C. 1986

R.J. Gettens & G.L. Stout, *Painting Materials. A short encyclopaedia,* New York 1966

C.V. Horie, *Materials for Conservation,* Oxford 1994

H. Kühn, e.a., 'Farbmittel, Buchmalerei, Tafel- und leinwandmalerei', in: *Reclams Handbuch der Künstlerischen Techniken,* Band I, Stuttgart 1984

M. Matteini & A. Moles, *Naturwissenschaftliche Untersuchungsmethoden in der Restaurierung,* translated by A. Burmester, München 1990

J.S. Mills & P. Smith (ed.s), *Cleaning, Retouching and Coatings,* Preprints of the IIC Brussels Congress London 1990

J.M. Montias, *Vermeer and his Milieu, A web of social history,* Princeton 1989

K. Nicolaus, *Het schilderij: Materiaal, techniek – behoud,* De Bilt 1980

H.P. Schramm & B. Hering, *Historische Malmaterialien und ihre Identifizierung,* Berlin 1989

H. von Sonnenburg, in: 'Technical Comments', *The Metropolitan Museum of Art Bulletin* (1973) 31

V. Todd (ed.), *Dirt and Pictures Separated,* UKIC, London 1990

A.K. Wheelock Jr., *Jan Vermeer,* New York 1988

Restoration project leader
Jørgen Wadum

Restoration of *The Girl with a Pearl Earring*
Nicola Costaras
Jørgen Wadum

Restoration of the *View of Delft*
Luuk Struick van der Loeff

Documentation
Romy Buchheim

Photography
Ed Brandon, Han Geene, Lilian Philips,
Luuk Struick van der Loeff, Jørgen Wadum

Technical imaging
Professor JRJ van Asperen de Boer, Karin Groen, DSM,
Doerner Institute Munich

Text
Jørgen Wadum

Editor
René Hoppenbrouwers

Co-authors
René Hoppenbrouwers and Luuk Struick van der Loeff

Translation
TechTrans: Hans van Bemmelen, Susan Hunt

Design
Jan Johan ter Poorten and Cees de Jong, V+K Design

Lithography and printing
Kunstdrukkerij Mercurius-Wormerveer

© V+K Publishing/Inmerc, Wormer
Mauritshuis, The Hague

ISBN 90 66 11 0341
NUGI 921